Macrame

Learn How to Make Basic Macrame with Step by Step Guide

DEDICATION

Contents

Basic Macrame Knots And Projects

Basic Macrame Knots

Basic Macrame Knots And Projects

Lark's Head Knot

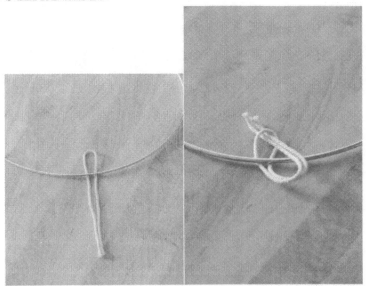

Basic Macrame Knots And Projects

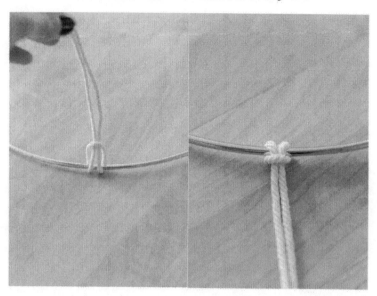

The Lark's Head Knot is one of the most basic knots in Macrame. In fact, almost every beautiful piece of finished macrame you see starts with this knot.

The Lark's head knot is used to attach your cording to your ring, dowel or handle when starting a macrame project.

Start by folding your piece of macrame cord in half.

See that little loop? Place that loop under your ring or dowel.

3

Basic Macrame Knots And Projects

Now fish the ends of the cording through that loop.
Pull tight and you have your lark's head knot!

Square Knot

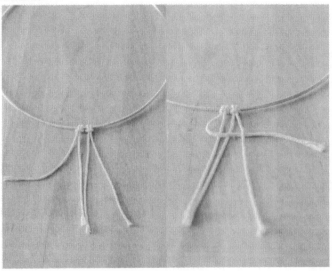

Basic Macrame Knots And Projects

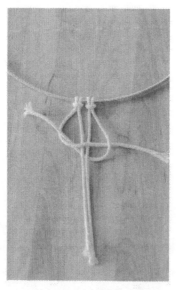

There are essentially two parts to the square knot. You have to complete one side (also called a half square knot) and then the other side (also called a right half square knot) to make the full square knot.

Start with two Lark's head Knots.

There should be a total of 4 macrame cords there.

We are going to take the outer left cord and cross it over the two middle cords.

Now take the outer right cord and place it on top of the left cord and UNDER the two middle cords.

Loop it through the hole on the left side.

Basic Macrame Knots And Projects

Now pull tight without letting your cords twist.

Yay! You now have ONE side of your square knot done. You have now completed a half square knot.

Now, let's do the other side...

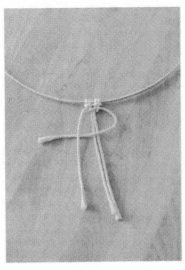

Basic Macrame Knots And Projects

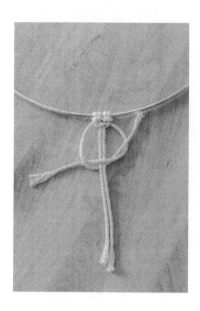

Basic Macrame Knots And Projects

You should still see your 4 cords there – got it? Good.

Take the outer RIGHT cord and cross it over the two middle cords.

Take the outer left cord and place it on top of the left cord and UNDER the two middle cords.

Loop it through the hole on the right side.

Basic Macrame Knots And Projects

Now pull your cords tight. Your Right Half Square Knot is complete.

You have completed the full square knot.

When you repeat this knot over and over again (in rows or sinnets) – you end up with a beautiful pattern of tightly weaved or netted cording.

This photo below is an alternating square knot.

Basic Macrame Knots And Projects

This is more of a wider pattern. I love alternating square knots with

Basic Macrame Knots And Projects

even spacing in between the knots.

Basic Macrame Knots And Projects

To make the alternating square knot as I did above, start with 4 Lark's head knots (there will be 8 total cords).

Make a square knot with four left side cords.

Make a square knot with the four right side cords.

Make a square knot with the four middle cords. (Push away the outer two cords on the left and right side to make it easier.)

Continue working this pattern, left, right, middle, left, right, middle.

Make sure to pull your cords tight without any twisting.

Basic Macrame Knots And Projects

Half Hitch

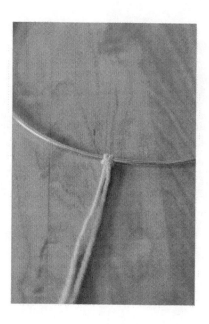

Basic Macrame Knots And Projects

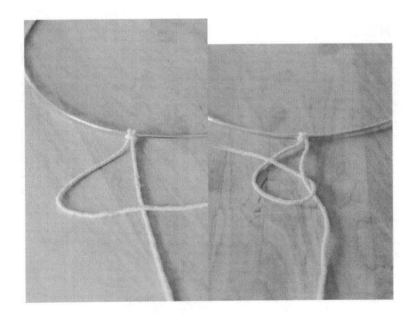

Basic Macrame Knots And Projects

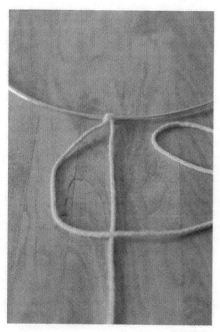

To me, a half hitch is simply your basic knot.   Follow these steps …

Start with a Lark's head knot.

Take one cord and make a number 4.

Loop that cord through the "4" hole and pull tight.

You made a half hitch knot!

Double Half Hitch

A double half hitch knot is just a half hitch knot repeated a second

Basic Macrame Knots And Projects

time.

Start with a Lark's head knot.

Take one cord and make a number 4.

Loop that cord through the "4" hole and pull tight.

Make another number 4 using the same cord you used before.

Loop it through the hole of the "4" and pull tight.

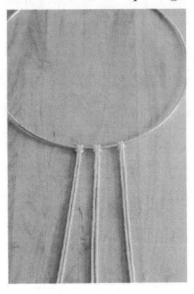

Basic Macrame Knots And Projects

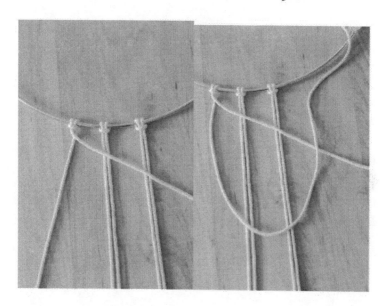

See that diagonal pattern I made? You can make this by doing a repeat of double half hitch knots. (See photo above)

Here's how to make it:

Start with 3 or more Lark's head knots. For this example – we are using 3 Lark's Head knots. There is a total of 6 cords.

Take the outer left cord and place it diagonally across all the other 5 cords. This cord is your filler cord. The direction and placement of this outer left cord will determine the pattern. So just make sure it's

Basic Macrame Knots And Projects

placed the way you want over your cords.

Working left to right, make a double half hitch knot with the second cord.

Pull your cord tight. Ensure your outer left cord is still placed diagonally over the cords.

Now make a double half hitch knot with the third cord.

Now make a double half hitch knot with the fourth cord.

And keep going until you reach the last cord on the right side. You will see your diagonal pattern of knots.

Now, you are going to repeat steps 2-7 but this time working right to left. So place the outer right cord diagonally over the other cords.

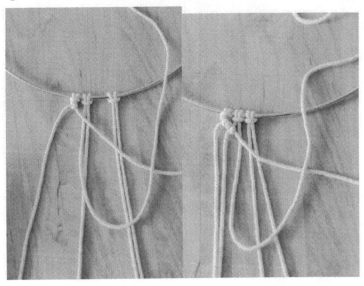

Basic Macrame Knots And Projects

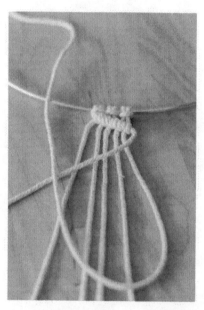

You can also make a horizontal line of double half hitch knots (just go horizontal instead of diagonal with that first cord).

There are variations to the half hitch knots, (like triple half hitch knots), but even with these basic half hitch knots, you can make great patterns.

19

Basic Macrame Knots And Projects

Spiral Knot

I think the Spiral knot is one of the prettiest knots. And fortunately – it's one of the easiest too.

You already know how to do the spiral knot.

It's just a repeat pattern of half square knots (first half of a square

Basic Macrame Knots And Projects

knot) or half hitch knots.

Instead of switching to the right side to complete the square knot, you just keep working that left side. The macrame will naturally spiral. Just go with it.

To make a thicker version of the spiral knot, start with 2 Lark's Head knots.

To make a single version – start with 1 Lark's Head knot and make a repeat pattern of half hitch knots. Again – your macrame will naturally start to twist. This is the pattern on the far right below.

Basic Macrame Knots And Projects

The trickiest part of this knot is keeping the pattern going the right way when it starts to twist.

Basic Macrame Knots And Projects

Simple DIY Macrame Feathers

Basic Macrame Knots And Projects

Materials Needed

Macrame Cording – I used this one

Sharp Scissors – I used these fabric scissors

Stiffening Spray

Wire Brush

Tape Measure – to measure your cords

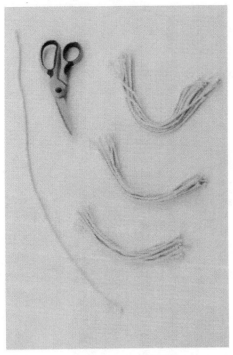

Keep your cords organized and separated by length. Look – they are

Basic Macrame Knots And Projects

smiling at you! ☺

cut the following lengths of cord :

Large Feather – 1 – 24" inch piece, 10 – 12" inch pieces, 10 – 10" pieces, 10 – 8" pieces (31 total cords)

Smallish Feathers – 1- 12" inch piece, 6 – 6" inch pieces, 4 – 4" pieces, 4 – 3" pieces (15 total cords)

If you look at a feather – it is slightly wider at the base and gets skinnier toward the top. So we start with the longest cords first, then go to our medium-sized cords and finally end with the smallest cords.

Here's how you Make Feathers ...

Basic Macrame Knots And Projects

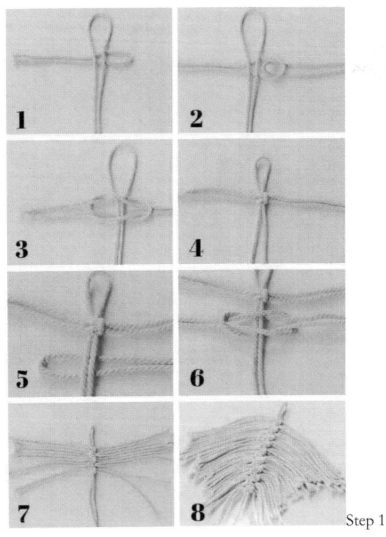

Step 1

First, take your longest cord and fold it in half. For the large feather,

Basic Macrame Knots And Projects

this is the 24" piece. For the smallish feathers, this is the 12" one. This long piece is the "spine" of our feather. Then, take one of your longest cords and fold it in half. Place it perpendicular under the spine of your feather to the right as shown in picture #1 above.

Step 2

Take another one of your longest cords and fold it in half. Pull the loop part through the loop of the first cord you laid down (not the spine). Pull it through over the spine part of your feather.

Step 3

Take the ends of the first cord and pull them through the loop of the second cord. I hope this is making sense! You should have something that looks like picture #3.

Step 4

Now pull the cords tight! Yay! You made your first knot on the spine.

Step 5

Now we are going to repeat Steps 1-4, but we are going to switch

Basic Macrame Knots And Projects

sides. So take another one of the longest cords and fold in half. Place your loop on the left side (instead of the right) as shown in picture #5.

Step 6

Now take another cord, fold in half, and loop it through the loop on the left. Pull the ends up and through this loop. Look at picture #6 for reference.

Step 7

Pull each cord tight and keep alternating sides – right, left, right, left, etc. Once you use up all your longest cords, switch to your medium cords, following this same process. Then switch to your smallest cords.

Step 8

You should have something that looks like picture #8!

Basic Macrame Knots And Projects

Step 9

Once you use up all your cords, you will brush them out with your wire brush to create the strands. Hold the spine at the same time so you don't pull off any knots.

Basic Macrame Knots And Projects

Tip : If you find that your spine still extends pretty long, you can just trim it to even it up.

You can also unravel the cords first with your fingers. I brushed them out on top of an old towel so I didn't damage any surfaces. I had to brush pretty hard to get these nice strands!

Flip your feather over and brush both sides to ensure all the cords all brushed out.

Basic Macrame Knots And Projects

Brush out cording for fringe

Step 10

After you brush it all out, take your scissors and trim up your feather.

Step 11

Spray your feather with stiffening spray to stiffen up the feather so it lays flat when it's hanging.

Follow this same process to make the smaller feathers or any size you want!

Basic Macrame Knots And Projects

You can use these DIY macrame feathers to make a cool wall hanging too. All you need to do is grab a dowel or stick and attach the stiffened feathers. A wall hanging won't work without stiffening them up though, the feathers will be too floppy.

You could also make a cool framed picture out of them, which is what I plan to do!

Basic Macrame Knots And Projects

Modern DIY Macrame Wall Hanging

33

Basic Macrame Knots And Projects

Materials Needed

Macrame Rope – I used this 4mm rope – You will need (twelve) 12 – 16' (as in feet) cords. Remember this is a long wall hanging that's why we need longer cords. You will also need 1 shorter piece of cording to serve as your hanger. Just tie it on there with a simple knot on either end.

A dowel or stick – I used a long knitting needle (haha). As long as it's straight and sturdy and the length you need- work with what you got!

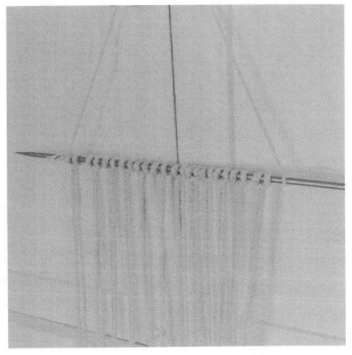

I'm so excited to be presenting you with this first macrame project.

Basic Macrame Knots And Projects

This wall hanging pattern was made using the following basic macrame knots:

Reverse Lark's Head Knot

Square Knot and Alternating Knot

Double Half Hitch Knot

Tutorial for DIY Macrame Wall hanging

Here's the step-by-step tutorial for this wall hanging.

Basic Macrame Knots And Projects

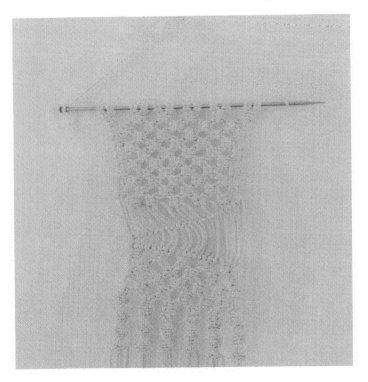

The first thing you want to do is knot some cord around each end of your dowel. This will serve as the hanger for our project. It's much easier to make a macrame wall hanging when it's hanging rather than laying down flat. You can hang this from cabinet knobs, doorknobs, a wreath hanger or even a picture hanger. Just make sure it's sturdy!

Start by folding your 16' cords in half. Make sure the ends are even.

Basic Macrame Knots And Projects

Place the loop of the cord under your dowel and thread the ends of the rope through the loop. Pull tight. That's your first Reverse Lark's Head knot. (Refer to basic macrame knots for help).

Repeat Step #3 with the remaining 11 cords. It should now look like the photo above.

Make 2 rows of Square Knots first. (Refer to basic macrame knots for help).

Now make 2 rows of Alternating Square Knots.

Now make another 2 rows of Square knots.

Continue to follow this pattern (2 rows of square knots, 2 rows of alternating square knots) until you have a total of 10 rows.

Basic Macrame Knots And Projects

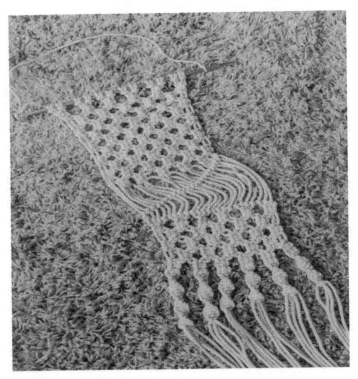

Working from left to right – make double half hitch knots in a diagonal pattern across your piece. (Refer to basic macrame knots for help).

Now, working from right to left – make double half hitch knots in a diagonal pattern across your piece.

You should have worked your way back over to the left side!

Continue the pattern of 2 rows of Square knots then 2 rows of

38

Basic Macrame Knots And Projects

Alternating Square Knots until you have a total of 4 rows.

Make 2 more rows of square knots. We are going to finish the wall hanging with a set of spiral knots – which is basically just a series of half square knots (or left side square knots). (Don't complete the right side of the square knot, just make left side square knots over and over again and it will spiral for you.) (Refer to basic macrame knots for help).

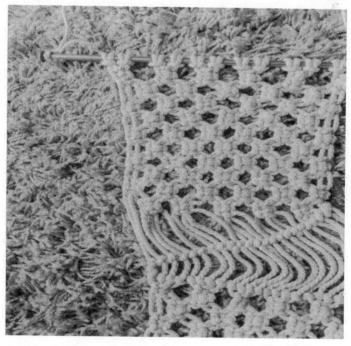

I made a total of 13 half square knots to create this spiral.

Finally – I trimmed the bottom cords into a straight line.

Basic Macrame Knots And Projects

Total dimensions for my wall hanging are 6.5" wide by 34 " long.

Basic Macrame Knots And Projects

Pretty Macrame Mason Jars

Basic Macrame Knots And Projects

Here's what you Need

Macrame Cord – this is the same one I've been using all week! (yep – you can make all these beautiful things with this one batch of rope)

Scissors

Mason Jars – I had one larger one with a handle and one regular size.

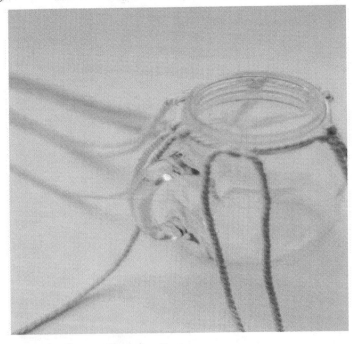

Macrame Mason Jars – Step by Step

Let's start by cutting the cords we need.

Basic Macrame Knots And Projects

For this project – I made two jars. One regular-sized mason jar and one larger sized mason jar with a handle.

I cut the cords all the same lengths for both jars – you will have to cut off some excess on the regular-sized jar at the end. But it's always better to have too much cord than too little!

Create a macrame mason jar

The larger mason jar has a pattern of one alternating square knot all the way around

For each jar, you will cord that is 6 feet long each.

Basic Macrame Knots And Projects

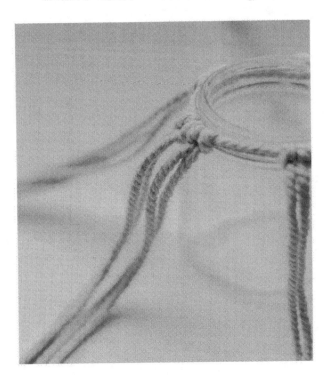

You will need 6 cords for the larger jar, and 8 cords for the regular jar.

The patterns for each jar vary slightly:

The larger mason jar with handle (known as Larger in this tutorial): The Pattern is one alternating square knot all the way around.

Regular Mason Jar (known as Regular in this tutorial): The Pattern is 2 square knots followed by sets of 2 alternating square knots all the

Basic Macrame Knots And Projects

way around.

To begin each jar : Regular: Take two of your 6 ft cords and wrap them around the lip of the jar – secure them with a single square knot. Larger: Take one of your 6 ft cords and wrap them around the lip of the jar – secure with a regular knot.

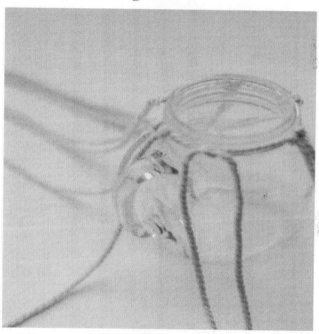

2. Attach the rest of your cords: Regular: Take the rest of your 6 cords and attach them to your jar using reverse lark's head knots. Larger: Take the rest of your 5 cords and attach them to your jar using reverse lark's head knots. Evenly space the knots all around the

Basic Macrame Knots And Projects

lip of the jar.

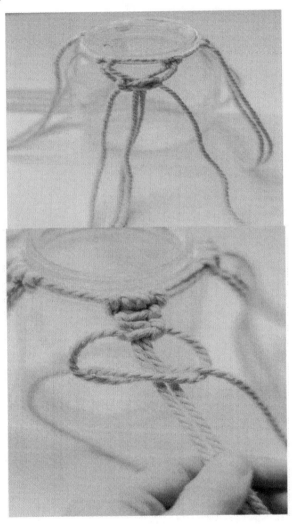

Basic Macrame Knots And Projects

3. Tie Square Knots: Regular: Make 2 square knots all the way around. Larger: Make a row of 1 alternating square knot all the way around the jar.

Basic Macrame Knots And Projects

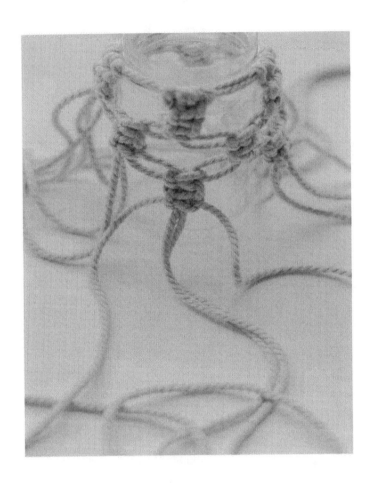

Basic Macrame Knots And Projects

4. Continue the Pattern down the jar: Regular: Now make a row of 2 alternating square knots. Continue these rows of alternating square knots until you get to the bottom of the jar. Larger: Continue with another row of alternating square knots all the way around. Do this until you reach the bottom of the jar.

Basic Macrame Knots And Projects

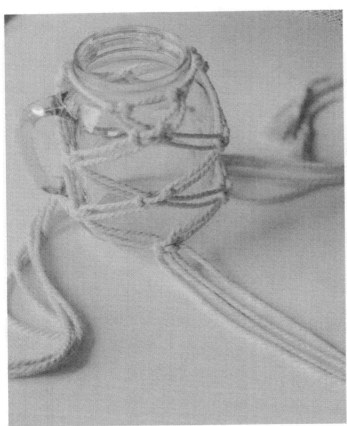

Hint : Do you have a handle on your jar? Just work around it by making your knots around or through the handle.

Basic Macrame Knots And Projects

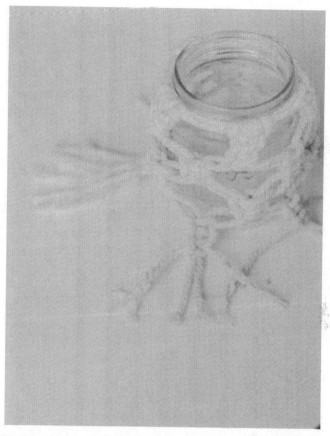

5. Finish the Jar: Regular/Larger: When you get to the bottom of the jar, cut off some excess rope but leave a bit there and comb them out for a fringe look.

Basic Macrame Knots And Projects

That's it! How pretty do these look?

I put some tea candles in my macrame mason jars for a nice glow!

Basic Macrame Knots And Projects

I wanted my jars to still be visible so that's why I chose spaced out, alternating square knots.

However – if you really wanted to cover the whole jar, you could use

Basic Macrame Knots And Projects

smaller sized rope and make really tightly weaved alternating square knots. Hmm, maybe I'll work on a version of that to add here.

Wouldn't this be a cute favor or housewarming gift? Fill it with a beautiful candle and tie a gift tag. The presentation is uniquely cool.

And, if you have a coastal vibe going on in your home, these would look amazing added to your decor. Maybe on a bookshelf or a side table.

Basic Macrame Knots And Projects

DIY Macrame Pillow

Basic Macrame Knots And Projects

Materials Needed

Macrame Cord

Scissors

Sewing Machine/Thread (optional)

Pillow cover and insert

Dowel or Stick

Tape Measure

Basic Macrame Knots And Projects

DIY Macrame Pillow Tutorial

For this Pillow, you can either start with a pillow cover you already have or make a quick envelope pillow cover. But don't make it just yet – see Step 5 first. I made a quick pillow cover out of this drop cloth. It ended up matching the rope perfectly and it looks great. If you really want to make the macrame pop, however, choose a contrasting color for your cover.

Basic Macrame Knots And Projects

For reference, my cover is 20×20 inches. You want to make sure your macrame pattern will cover your pillow — but the good news is you can stretch it to fit if need be.

Step 1

Cut your cords! You will need 16 – 12 foot cords to make this pattern. (And you will have a bit of excess depending how long you want your fringe).

Step 2

Attach all 16 of your cords to your dowel using reverse lark head knots. Refer to the Basic Macrame Knots Post to see how to do this knot.

Step 3

The pattern for this cover is just rows of 1 alternating square knot. I left a bit of space in between each knot — about half an inch for reference. Plus, leaving a bit of spacing helps the project go that much faster.

You want to continue to make your alternating square knots until you reach near the bottom of 20 inches. Use your tape measure to keep

Basic Macrame Knots And Projects

track of where you are.

Once you reach the bottom, make a two horizontal rows of (left to right, then right to left) or double half hitch knots.

Step 4

Now that we are finished with the pattern, cut the excess off the bottom, but leave a bit of fringe hanging – I left about 5 inches or so. You can leave more or less, totally up to you.

Now you are going to either detach from your dowel or just cut it off at the

Step 5 : How do I attach this to my pillow cover?

Here's how you can attach your macrame pattern to your pillow. If you are making a cover yourself, before you sew it up – you are going to basically line up the pattern to the front of your cover leaving the cut ends over hanging the top a bit.

Basic Macrame Knots And Projects

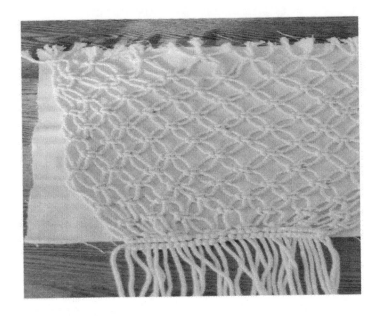

Basic Macrame Knots And Projects

Lay the back piece over top of your cover and macrame pattern- right sides facing together – basically you are making a sandwich here and the macrame is considered the "meat".

Now just sew the top seam of your pillow cover – go over the ropes too! It takes a bit of finesse, but you can do it. I pinned it to hold everything together.

To sew the rest of your cover, shove the macrame pattern inside your pillow and sew the rest of the seams as normal.

Flip it right side out. You should now have your macrame pattern

Basic Macrame Knots And Projects

attached to your pillow at the top (coming out from in between your seam).

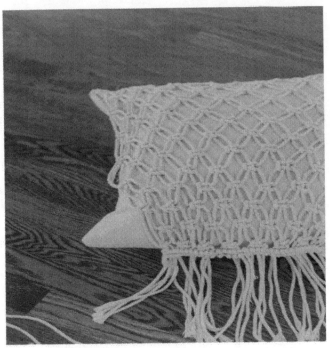

To attach the rest of the cover – I took another piece of macrame cord and tied a simple knot in the back. You will never really see the back so who cares. I looped this cord in and out of square knots. This will not only help stretch your pattern out, but it will secure it down towards the bottom.

Basic Macrame Knots And Projects

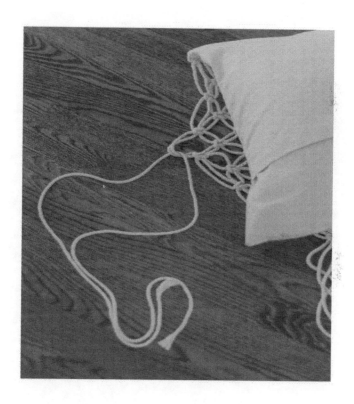

Basic Macrame Knots And Projects

Basic Macrame Knots And Projects

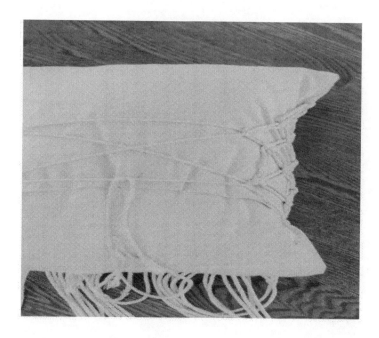

And that's it! Your fringe will be left hanging from the bottom.

Basic Macrame Knots And Projects

Made in the USA
Middletown, DE
06 October 2023

40346221R00043